EBURY PRESS
UNSUNG

Arunoday Singh was born in February 1983, in Delhi. He grew up in Bhopal, where his parents live, deep in the woods, by a lake. At the age of seven, he went to Kodaikanal International School, in the deep south of India. In the spring of 2000, he left for America for the first time, to attend Brandeis University near Boston. He graduated summa cum laude with a bachelor's in English literature, creative writing and journalism. He is an actor by primary profession, though—because nothing can be easy with this one. He currently lives in Mumbai, by the Arabian Sea, trying to act, pretending to write.

POEMS

unsung

arunoday singh

EBURY
PRESS

An imprint of Penguin Random House

EBURY PRESS

USA | Canada | UK | Ireland | Australia
New Zealand | India | South Africa | China

Ebury Press is part of the Penguin Random House group of companies
whose addresses can be found at global.penguinrandomhouse.com

Published by Penguin Random House India Pvt. Ltd
4th Floor, Capital Tower 1, MG Road,
Gurugram 122 002, Haryana, India

First published in Ebury Press by Penguin Random House India 2022

Copyright © Arunoday Singh 2022

All rights reserved

10 9 8 7 6 5 4 3 2 1

ISBN 9780670095735

Typeset in Baskerville by Manipal Technologies Limited, Manipal

www.penguin.co.in

For my father,
Who gave me spirit.
For my mother,
Who gave me grace.
For my sisters,
Who give me
Music and joy, while
Laughing in my face.

I am because of you.

Contents

About the Cover   ix

Introduction   xi

Wind: Songs of the Lost   3

Stone: Songs of Stillness   21

Water: Songs of Hurt and Healing   47

Flame: Songs of Movement   73

Spirit: Songs of Light and Dark, of Me and You   99

Acknowledgements   159

About the Cover

The shell on the cover, designed by the lovely Antra K, is from an organism called the nautilus, one of the oldest surviving creatures in the ocean. Older than the dinosaurs. Far, far older than us.

As it grows, it builds larger and larger chambers in its shell. You would have seen its cross section many times. It's one of the best examples of the awesome symmetry and mathematical precision that can be found in nature. The older chambers are not discarded or left unused. They are filled with gas, which the nautilus uses to manipulate its buoyancy, draining or flooding them as needed, rising and sinking.

It is thought sacred because its structure is based on the golden ratio, which can be found in all living things: the shape of our galaxy, of hurricanes, in the arrangement of seeds in the sunflower, in cauliflower and pine cones. (Google for more information on it. And you really should. It's fascinating.)

It is considered a powerful symbol of growth and renewal, with its methodical, ordered expansion. As the nautilus grows, it expands its shell to precisely contain and protect. No more, no less. This is particularly symbolic of spiritual evolution. It represents order in a world thought ruled by chaos. An order that is built on the past, on the bones of its own history.

The 'Nautilus' is what Captain Nemo named his vessel in *Twenty Thousand Leagues Under the Sea*. Among the first books I remember loving in the way you only ever seem to love great books.

I found a nautilus shell the first time I ever went snorkelling, in Lakshadweep as a boy. It felt like finding sunken treasure. It sits on my desk even today.

The fisherman who was ferrying us between islands told me that all shells sing the songs of the ocean. But only the nautilus holds the ones that remain unsung.

This book is my nautilus shell. It contains all the songs I never got to sing, held in all the chambers that I used to fill. And I know that I am but the wave, meant to carry all these songs, to you.

Introduction

I've been waiting for you my entire life. Dreaming of the moment you'd stand before me, and I could finally say all the things I was destined to tell you. Through my loneliest, most difficult noons and nights, I drew hope from an odd, but utter certainty that one day, we *will* speak.

Now you're finally, suddenly, here. It seems so unexpectedly unreal, that I have been struck dumb. I honestly don't know how to begin to write an introduction to a book I've only ever dreamt about. I'm giddy and incoherent with joy.

Deep breath.

Smother shiver.

Deeper breath.

There we go.

Hi.

Welcome to the psycho-paleontological record of the last, particularly tumultuous period of my life. These poems are samples of what I felt, what broke, what burnt, and what managed to survive enough to heal. This is evidence of the journey I made through depression and all my collected angst (which was sizeable indeed), into a quieter, more solid sense of joy. Battered and bruised, but wiser and gentler and much, much happier.

It's everything that I've felt and seen of heartbreak, healing and hope. I'm not trying to gild this with fake grandeur. I've been writing as long as I can remember. (I'll tell you the story of why. It's a good one. There's a girl in it.) In that time, my writing and my voice have worn many a disguise. I was always better at being somebody else.

I have a brain that feels like a hurricane on a good day. Minimalism is meditation for me. It took me a while to figure that out. My earlier work read like a thesaurus vomited on the page. I had to learn that knowing more doesn't mean understanding more. That what was propelling me to write, wasn't a desire to impress or gain fame, but to understand my own confusion and to convey everything I found to be true. To share and comfort. To reach out and hold the hand of my readers, and give them whatever help I could, to make them see that they weren't alone either physically or in their emotions. I didn't want to awe people with my inner Stephen Fry (pale shadow, of course), I just wanted to tell them these simple things that helped me, in as minimalist and accessible a form as I could.

These poems may seem simple, but I hope you can see that they're simple like a stone is simple. A stone is exactly what it is supposed to be, in as simple a shape as nature allowed it to assume. A stone will never question its purpose. It is meant to be a stone. Beneath everything else, nothing other than itself. My effort with these poems in particular, has been to brush off all detritus and clutter my writing used to be covered with, and still is, albeit to lesser degrees. To leave just the stone.

It's taken me many years of crippling insecurity to stop trying to write like any of the people I admire; to find my own voice. To actually step out of the way of judging myself so harshly and approach the writing process like a cobbler making a shoe, not a kid thinking the only choices were to write something better than *For Whom the Bell Tolls* on his first try, or never write at all.

I used to spend an inordinate amount of time just staring at the blank page before me. Feeling a strange, double-edged panic; I haven't written a thing, and I can't write a single thing that won't be nauseatingly mediocre, at best. So there I sit, staring at nothing, writing nothing. I can't quite capture the inner imagery of the frustration. It's as if I were trying to perfectly describe and conjure the full awe of an ocean, by drawing with raindrops on a pane of glass.

It's been a hell of a trek to the point where I don't worry about whether I will be able to do the ocean any justice. I don't need to describe it. You're in it too, just by virtue of being human. The poem is just the stone I throw into your water. Because the ripples are the point.

What a long-winded ramble. I panicked. It happens. Anyway. On to the matter at hand.

You hold in your hand my first book of poetry. Just saying that makes me Grinch-grin, for joy, of course. But just as wide. And to some people, just as disconcerting.

I was always fairly good at most subjects during my school/college years, but English classes were always where my heart would be gladdest. Well, that and theatre/acting, which were only enhanced by my love for words. I had magnificent teachers: Pramod Menon, Asha Hariharan, William Flesch, Bernd Pflug.

I started scribbling in journals, in margins, on napkins. Not for any directed aim or purpose, nor because I possessed any talent for it. It just helped a shy kid learn to bring the whirlwind of his mind to some sort of order, even if to a laughable degree. It felt like talking to someone. I would read what I wrote as if someone else had sent the words to me. I wrote to myself. I wrote for myself. Writing, even the painful, cringeworthy, adolescent kind, sustained me. I didn't judge it. (Well that's a lie, I judge it constantly. But that's more judging that it's me writing, rather than the writing itself, if that makes sense). I never judged the words. They just were what they were.

I started writing poetry, to impress a girl (because, of course). I grew late, was awkward and shy, and (always) wonderfully odd. Boarding school was not a pleasant jaunt by any stretch.

She was a teenager on the cusp of an adulthood worthy of a goddess, and popular and interesting. She was always laughing and running and dancing. I called her Pocahontas in my head. I was always just brooding or reading. I had zero game. I didn't even know that there was such a thing as 'game'. I thought you could like someone strongly enough and the power of that affection and regard makes them like you too. Like a magic spell.

Poetry seemed to work in the books and movies I loved. Evidence showed that it played a big part in successful romancing and wooing. And I loved words, and I felt they loved me back. I always had more words in me than the people around me. Words could be my secret weapon. So, at fourteen years old, I started trying to write love sonnets worthy of Neruda for my teenage muse.

The world should rejoice that not a single copy or record of anything I wrote during this phase exists. No one deserves to be subjected to such horror. Definitely not the aforementioned goddess. She never got any of the poems I sent to her, through my roommate (who was her science lab partner). He pretended to give them to her and wrote fake replies back, lightly dusted with some scent that I will forever associate with her and those days.

Bastard.

But he did ensure that she never read any of them. Epic fail would have ensued. Well, I failed at wooing her anyway, but at least she never laughed in my face holding one of my poems, surrounded by all her attractive, popular friends. Ah, teenagers.

That experience ensured that, for whatever I wrote in the future, I'd be wordless and worthless without a muse.

For the words to feel like they flowed. For one day, the Muse to finally read my words, and fall head over chappals in love with me.

A couple of gloriously disastrous relationships and one imploded marriage later, I've finally stopped looking for muses (God, I hope so). I've learnt that if I am just honest with myself, and unafraid to look at who and what I am in its entirety, to be earnestly introspective, the words still come in waves. As long as I sit at the desk and go to work every day.

Now I write like a bird flies. Because that's just how it was intended to move. That's why it has wings. This is not to claim some sort of divine beauty in this ability, nor in the quality of the writing. It's just how it feels. Just how it is, for me. I'm just describing the symptoms to you, doctor.

I take the same amount of time, I suppose, staring at an empty page when writing poetry as I do prose. It's just that, in the case of poetry, something else, outside of me, sends me the words. All I do is wait until they come, or write them down as soon as they do if I'm doing something else. I'll pull over on a highway to write. I stop halfway to boarding a flight to write. I have paused making out, to write something down before I lost it (and yes, thus lost the girl. Sigh.).

It is a condition.

Over the years, I have gotten comfortable and more at ease with writing and stopped trying to write something earth-shattering, and just concentrated on something simple and true. It was then, as I started to find my ease with it, that I started to notice something curious.

My favourite of my own poems are all elemental.

What do I mean by this? I mean literally, either with metaphors and analogies, sometimes in subtler ways, sometimes just in the flavour of the emotion they invoke, there are themes/suggestions of the primal elements of the universe: Wind, Water, Stone and Flame. And, of course, Spirit.

When I read deeper, I began to see there were clear connections between the element of the poem(s) I was writing, and my own emotional state at the time, or the time the poem was talking about. Even if not overtly or explicitly, I could sense their essence when I reread things I'd written, during my incessant tinkering sessions with the poems I've written, or while flipping through my notebooks full of fragments and disordered thoughts.

I remember my ex-wife, who studied Ayurveda, had told me about how that ancient science divides the body into these very elements, when trying to define and demarcate the humours and energies that flow through and make up the human body. Ayurveda believes that it is imbalances of these elements in us that lead to illnesses both physical and, to some degree, mental.

On a whim, at an Ayurvedic clinic in Goa, I once filled in an extensive questionnaire before my first consultation with a doctor. Based on my answers, the doctor explained how I, apparently, am a child of fire. There were all sorts of fascinating and frighteningly accurate inferences that she made about what might be happening with my system and what should ideally be the balance. For example, her test revealed that I had too much 'wind' in my system (no, not that kind, you absolute child . . . although, yeah that too). Fire does not do well with an excess of wind energy, in particular. It leads to a very chaotic and unsettled mind–body.

Chaotic and unsettled are mild adjectives to describe the invisible hell-scape that I was stumbling through in my mind, in those days. Much later, when I was glancing through my notebooks of that year, I read a lot of 'wind', 'lost', 'storm' in my scribblings. After that, I began paying attention to deeper impressions of the poems I wrote, especially after letting them sit in a drawer for months so I could come back to them fresh.

It wouldn't always be accurate or revelatory, but there was definitely a pattern and irrefutably, a connection. My emotional/mental state manifested throughout my work in the elemental imagery I used, without me even being conscious of it. I began to be able to better guess and gauge my own mental state and health, by seeing which element lurked in the poem. It was a whimsical quirk. Nothing spectacular or special, nothing planned, and certainly nothing used to steer how and what I wrote about. It would just be in the back of my mind, and beneath the poem.

Thus, when I was thinking of a way to structure this book, this system seemed obvious. The book is divided into five sections: Wind, Stone, Water, Flame and Spirit. Each element is associated with a specific overarching emotional state. They don't follow any pre-existing system, other than my whimsy, even if there might be any overlap with established practices. Because an element, or anything rather, is never just one single thing, one single connotation. I can go on for hours about all the other possible meanings an element can conjure, but these are my primary ones. Entirely, idiosyncratically mine.

Wind for being lost and unsettled.
Stone for stillness and meditation.
Water for cleansing and healing.
Flame for energy and action.
Spirit, further divided into Light and Dark, Me and You.

I hope you enjoy them. These are all like songs I wrote, that never got sung because I didn't have that talent. Much as sometimes we feel that we are songs, which the world will never sing. We will never be heard, never be known and admired. And we're afraid to treat ourselves as reverently, because we think it doesn't matter when it comes from oneself.

I've learnt that is not true. Every breath you take is singing your song out loud. And I can hear you just fine.

WIND

SONGS OF THE LOST

Whenever I think of a character in a book or a film who is lost/abandoned/stranded in an unknown, hostile place, there is often a description or depiction of the wind. As if losing one's way is akin to getting blown away by the breeze, a leaf destined to never again find its tree. In an un-still silence, or an unwelcome solitude, the only sound you hear is the sound of the wind. Carrying the whispers of the others lost like you.

There is something restless about the wind. It comes from nowhere and goes everywhere. It isn't constant in direction, force or temperature. It doesn't have an origin, nor a destination. It just races about.

It makes me restless. Even on a hot, dry day, when it arrives like the cool breath of a winter god, it still makes me feel like abandoning my skin and racing alongside it. Wherever it wants to go. Just take me along. It makes me feel like I'm going against my every atom by being where I am, by not racing heedless across the land.

When I was younger, I used to romanticize the idea of being a rambling man when I grew up; with a gypsy soul, born for leaving, as the Zac Brown Band song goes. To live a life as a carefree wanderer. Free as the breeze.

Now I have done my fair share of rambling . . . I was happy for some of it, but that restless wind in my heart never let me settle, geographically, in my heart/mind. I never felt I belonged anywhere. Even in my parents' home, which is by far my favourite place on the planet. I always carried a sense of being exiled from some mythic, amorphous place, where I was *supposed* to be, where I belonged. Like a pilgrim lost in a dust storm.

In times of distress, anger or anxiety, I hear it in my mind just as you hear the muted roar of the ocean, whipping along the shore, beneath all the other sounds crowding the beach. Even the quiet moments and still corners of my mind echo with it. I hear it like tinnitus. A whispered hissing in the back of my being.

You learn as you grow that although you should be grateful for the wind, and enjoy it, you cannot be like the wind. You need tethering. Everyone does, I think, at least to different degrees. To a person, to a calling, to a dream. To yourself, most of all. But the older I get, the more restless and blown about like an autumn leaf I feel.

And when I look around, a lot of people seem to be similarly afflicted.

Why are so many of us restless all the time? Is it because we're not living the lives we would choose, if we even knew? Social media doesn't help. The world is louder and more expensive, and money seems to buy less and only find its way to the people who don't need it at all.

All the while we are told to move or get left behind, to be go-getters, hustlers, workhorses, etc. Feeling more and more panicked, rooted in place, which is what makes the inner wind terrifying. Because it blows harder than ever. There is a storm contained inside you and no one around you can even tell how terrified and lonely it leaves you. Leaning away, head down, to keep from being swept away, from anywhere you think you can rest.

I have made an active and conscious effort to learn how to harness that breeze. Not to be free of it; I stopped trying to wrestle that Titan down a long time ago. I've just learned to be aware of it and when it rises or dies down. Because it also fills my sails. Because it keeps me moving, even when I don't want to. Because it leads me where I need to be, I think. All I've done is gotten better at manning the rudder and much less prone to seasickness.

So when that wind blows hard enough again, off again into the unknown I am blown.

01

Whisper it to me,
I promise, I won't
Tell a soul.
Just between
Me and you.
Just tell me if
There is something,
There, at the end of it,
Worth all that we
Are going through.

~

02

There are
Pieces of us,
Missing.
Pieces we lost
Somewhere
Along the way.
Who knows when.
Who knows where.
If only we
Could remember.
Or at least forget,
That we ever had them,
At all.

~

03

I know
The peaks.
I know
The troughs.
It's in those
Grey
In-betweens,
I am lost.

~

04

In thinking,
You are lost.
In thinking,
You can drown.
Only in silence,
Will you find,
What thinking keeps,
From being found.

~

05

It's a lonely walk,
Back to where
I was always
Meant to be.
But it's only
On this road,
I learnt lessons,
I didn't know
I needed.
Found things,
I didn't know
I had lost.

~

06

There must be
A sorrow,
I keep secret,
Even from me.
One day,
I will find
That sorrow,
And learn why
I ever
Hid it away.
On that day,
I will be ready,
For lasting joy.

~

07

Does the fire,
Ever learn,
What it means
To be still,
Or is that only
For the ash
To know?
Then I wonder
About my heart.
Then I fear
For us all.

~

08

We don't always know
What we want.
We don't always get
What we need.
Too many roads
Divided before us.
There were no signs
To help us decide.
We just found ourselves
Where we are,
At nothing like
A destination.
Looking back
To find some hint,
Of where we wanted to go.
Some trace
Of who we thought
We were going to be.
By now.

~

09

Where are you?
Trapped,
In someone else's dream?
Held hostage by
Someone else's promises,
More lost than you seem?
Why can't I find you?
What's taking so long?
Is everything all right?
Or does it all seem more
Than slightly wrong
In your life like in mine?
Is my destiny ahead of me,
Or have I left it behind?
Busy pretending I knew
Where I was heading,
When I knew I was
Just walking blind.
Find me. Please.
Before joy becomes
Just another
Hopeless quest.
We're running out of time.

~

10

We are shaped
Like pieces of clay.
Kneaded,
Spun,
Formed
Into function.
In a world
That knows
Nothing but thirst.
We are the ones
Who can hold
The water.
We are the cups
The world brings
To its lips.
But there are
More cracks now.
We are all
Running dry.

~

11

I wonder if
It ever strikes you
This feeling of being
Immense, yet unseen
At the same time.

Reaching out,
Bring to pull
The entire Universe
Towards your
Singularity.

That unfound
Event horizon,
Hidden deep in
The vast expanse
Of your heart.

Every breath
A cataclysm
No one else can feel.
Every ache an answer
No one wants to find.

We're tracing orbits
Around each other
In the cosmic dark.
Unable to escape
The Gravity.

The astrophysics
Of Love and Hurt.
Curving space-time
Around us.
Pulling us together
Ripping us apart.

~

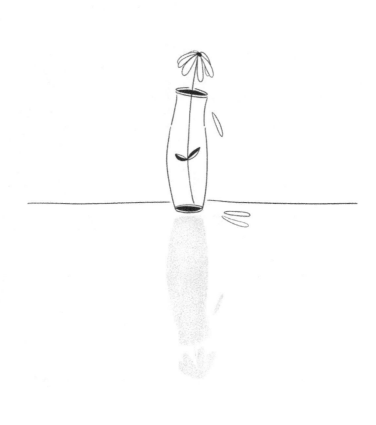

STONE

SONGS OF STILLNESS

A stone is such a simple thing. Like this stone in my hand, that I carried down from halfway up the Siachen glacier years ago. That I use as a paperweight on my desk. That I stare at as I meditate. Trying to find a still respite from my inner whirlwind, the search for which has been one of the great battles in my life.

I have always felt wind-tossed. I made my peace with the constant gale in my heart–mind. But I also knew if I didn't seek true calm, a way to find pockets of silence from the mental tumult, everything I liked about myself would be doomed. I would worry and overthink myself to an early grave. Definitely unhappy. Probably alone.

I'm not being dramatic. This was a coherent, crystal-clear alarm. My body's warning bell asking for self-preservation. I needed meditation, breathing exercises, yoga, anything. I needed to learn to be like a stone.

I began to understand why it was called grounding. And why adults spoke about it so much. As a youth, one can get confused by one's intelligence, merriment and vigour, with some sort of invincible shield against the world. Then you grow older, and the world really starts coming for you, and you see how adorably naive you were. But just knowing more doesn't help at all in dealing with emotions or struggles when they arrive like cyclones. The more spiritually shaken one is, regardless of how smart or successful you may be, the harder the banal apocalypses and earth-shattering trivialities hit.

I knew I had to first learn to be still. Before I could ever hope to soar. I would defy the hurricanes, and make myself a boulder. Until I learnt how to evolve.

01

There is a Silence,
That will descend
On your heart.
In which all things
Become clear.
You will live in it,
Breathe, and be
Free in it.
Into which
You'll die, and
Finally disappear.

~

02

Every sorrow,
Is eventually
Spoken,
That doesn't mean,
It is all you
Will ever feel.

Every spell,
Is eventually
Broken,
That doesn't mean
The magic
Wasn't real.

~

03

Why do we drown,
When we know
How to swim?
Why trudge, when
We know that
We can fly?
Why do we lose,
When there's no
Need to win?
Why do we fail,
When we don't
Have to try?

~

04

Dear Life,
You will never know,
Just how much hurt,
Is hidden behind
Our smiles.
Be gentle with us.
We're held together,
Barely,
If at all.
Still, we smile,
At you.
Still, we run,
To you,
Like children
At a carnival.
Be gentle.

~

05

For so far,
My eyes have
Searched.
For so long,
My heart has,
Kept faith.
How much more,
Do I have
To see?
How much longer,
Must I be made,
To wait?

So I reach out,
Because you hope
Something, is reaching
Back for you.
You reach,
Because,
You'd rather die,
Than live with,
Not having reached.
Not even having tried.

I will wait a lifetime.
If I must.
Like all of us
Have to.
Like all of us
Do.

~

06

Think of all
Your failures.
Relive
Every crushing
Defeat.
Your heart never
Failed you.
Here you are.
Smiling, striving.
Capable hands,
Stubborn feet.
You've survived,
Every ending.
Let no beginning
Find your heart
Weak.
Afraid,
Of breaking.
Dive in.
Leap about.
Make a mess.

Break it.
Your heart is a warrior.
I promise you,
It can take it.

~

07

Dear Goddess,
Send me a sign.
A fire by the road
A stele on the climb
A direction to travel
Shelter to find.
As I make my way
Word by weary word,
Line by bloody line
To that secret place
In that sacred time
Where all men are poets,
All pets speak in rhyme.
All cups hold coffee
All glasses have wine
All smiles stretch true
Every hand holds mine.

~

08

Love and joy,
Are not fragile,
Precious things,
To be kept
Locked away,
On a shelf.
Far from the pain,
And the blood.

They should be
Smeared
Across your lips,
Scarred
Into your skin.
Caked under
Your fingernails,
Like playground mud.

~

09

A few days,
A few years,
A few lifetimes,
Circling around.
With no idea what
We should be
Looking for.
Hoping, someone
Will let us know,
When it's been found.
So we can stop.
The trouble,
I think,
Is that we are
A little homeless,
In our souls.
Trees,
In the wind.
Trying,
Desperately,
To hold on
To their leaves.

~

10

It is not
For the threads,
To question,
The Weaver's will.
But to be woven,
And, to be still.
Yet,
Here we are,
Writhing . . .

~

11

We are embers
Of a greater fire.
Holding on
To the memory
Of when we burned,
Impossibly bright.
And though we
Have long sat
Dimming
In the dark,
We know
A wind will come,
To fan us aflame.
To make us rise,
Fill us with Light,
Again.

~

12

You're tearing
At the seams
Of all that
You've been.

Growing
A bigger heart.
Weaving
Thicker skin.

Becoming so
Much more, than
What you lost,
What you'll win.

You're learning
What to shed,
To make space
For the wings.

~

13

You can make
Your mind
A prison, or
Make of it,
A clear
Winter sky.
If you have
To be a stone.
Be a stone,
Learning
To fly.

~

14

Everything we cherish,
Is slowly dying
All on its own.
This little world will vanish,
The Sun will grow cold,
The Moon will drift all alone.
Gods will be banished,
Even our spirits
Will cease to roam.
How little these truths
Really matter,
When the ones we love,
Throw themselves into our arms,
Like soldiers coming home.

~

15

The flames leapt,
Then fell to the ground.
The smoke drifted on its way.
The embers sighed,
Laid their burdens down.
I feared Love had gone away.
For I was always told,
Love is a fire, that must burn.
But Love remained,
After the fire was gone.
Love stayed to play.
Drawing fewer eyes.
Singing softer songs.

~

16

There is a need,
That has become
A knocking
In my heart.
Every day I live,
In the hope,
That today,
At last,
I'll make it
To the door,
In time.

~

17

The Universe,
Is drifting apart.
The stars
Are ever fading.
The Light just
Cannot stay.
Still we chase it.
For we are made,
To live and dance
In endless sunset.
Holding tight to each other,
While everything
Slips away.

~

18

Between my breaths.
At the centre point
Between breathing out,
And breathing in,
There is a poem
That waits for me.
Where I am empty
Of the world,
Of every thought,
Except this poem,
That I'm meant to free.
At the still centre,
Of the cosmic dance
This poem
Waits for me.
To help me build
The final bridge,
From you to me.

~

19

The one
who lights the fire,
Cannot teach the fire
About the breeze.
Yet it always dances
When that breeze
Passes through.

The one
who loves me,
Cannot teach me
How to be free.
Yet I dance for her
In the cage
I was born into.

~

20

I am never
As still
As I am
Upon a shore.
With the surf
Gasping at my feet,
And the Sun
Dying on the horizon.
Standing at
The edge of everything.
Even me.

~

WATER

SONGS OF HURT AND HEALING

Wounds are first washed. The body is bathed before any major prayer or ritual. We bathe to cleanse both body and mind. We can feel it, the languor and the release from angst we get after a shower.

I remember reading that human beings find diamonds and other things that glint and glitter so attractive because they glisten and sparkle like the shimmer of sunlight on water. Which is something our brains have been evolutionarily hardwired to seek above all else. Water is life.

Fountains of youth. Healing waters. Summer rain. Lovers' sweat. Much more than half our bodies is water. We are made of it. We are conceived, gestate, and are born from water.

Coasts, beaches, riversides, lake shores are full of restless people seeking a moment of spiritual rest. They all come to seek it by the water. Cities grow around water. Growth is constant breaking and remaking. Where else would that be easiest but by water?

So now, the healing can begin. The wind is calm. You've learnt the lessons of Stone. Now break yourself. When the breaking is done, and everything is rubble and dust. Wash it clean. Begin again.

00

It's a simple truth,
Woven into your skin.
If it healed you,
Heals you,
Or will heal you,
Let it in.

~

01

In the end,
It's what you
Don't surrender,
That will drive
The demons
Away.

~

02

Uncuff me
From this flesh.
Untouch me
Leave me unfound.
Unblink me
From memory
Unthink me
Leave me unbound.
Unsay
Every word said.
Unhear me,
Unchain me from
The sound,
Of my name.
Unwrite me
From these pages.
Unspeak me.
Unblame me
For the pride
And the shame,
Of being alive.

~

03

I swear,
I was infinite,
Just a moment ago.
What is this form
I have taken?
Where is this place,
I have awoken?
I swear
I was infinite,
Just, a moment ago.
Strangest thing.

~

04

I don't care,
How often
My faith
Is tested,
I know Love
Is worship.
I will always
Believe.

Even when
I'm terrified,
It's just some
Hopeless quest.
And all that
I have left
To believe in,
Is me.

~

05

Some days
I'm brimful,
Others,
I'm naught
But dust.
Those
Are the days
I can't go on.
Those are the days
I must.

~

06

I wish
I could
Return.
Before
The damage,
I cannot
Remember
Taking,
Made me
What I am
Today.
I wish
I could
At least
Get a peek,
At who
I might
Have been.
Had the damage
Not had
Its say.

~

07

Befriend your demons.
Admire your scars in the light.
Take pride in your bruises.
Smile through the blood that flows.
Hold tight this freedom,
You are as light
As free as a kite.
You could have quit,
Any time you chose.
But every time you were
Knocked down.
Was every time that you rose.

~

08

Here we are,
Pretending
We aren't fragile.
Waiting to be
Spoon-fed
Salvation.
Why don't we
Cry out?
Why can't we
Just shatter
Into a million pieces?
Let it break
Our minds.
Only then
Will we find
The strength of us,
In the pieces
The breaking
Leaves behind.

~

09

As a child,
I remember
Learning
There were seeds,
That needed fire
To bring them
To life.
They needed
To pass through fire,
To begin yearning,
To be trees.

As a man
I have learnt,
Life is fire,
And my heart,
To my delight,
Is such a seed.
I am no longer
Afraid,
Of burning.

~

10

We only truly
Understand
Each other,
By our sorrows.
For we know,
Without
The black sky,
We couldn't
Even see
The stars.
We may find
Comfort
In laughter,
But we find
Kinship,
In scars.

~

11

I once
Heard Leonard say,
'In life, at some point,
The accumulation
Of defeats becomes
Significant.'
I've learnt,
The thing to remember,
The thing to believe,
Is despite your defeats,
Your heart's strong enough,
To reach down,
And pull you back,
To muddied feet.
You have to break,
To learn you can thrive,
Amidst the breaking.
You have to give,
To learn to survive,
The endless taking.

~

12

We are
Pulled apart,
Not to leave us,
Threadbare,
Or make us,
Incomplete.
But to teach us,
To let us finally see,
As we knit ourselves
Back together,
There are threads
And pieces that
We no longer need.

~

13

This is my pen,
My answer to the crime.
This is my poem,
To wrap hope in rhyme.
This is my cigarette,
To burn away the time.
This is my heart,
The wreckage left behind.
This is my smile
That says I'll be just fine.

~

14

God can hear me,
Joy lasts forever.
Sunsets melt like hearts.
Nights are a treasure.
Traffic cannot find me here,
Everything is good for me.
There are no other people,
But those happy and free.
No work is unworthy,
And we all live by the Sea.
No nightmares for my Darling.
No worry lines on her face.
The sorrows that do find me,
Slip away, without a trace.
I'm the hero of this story,
Though the world waits
To have its way
With me again.
I'm the hero of this story.
Until I lay down my pen.

~

15

When I am troubled,
I imagine myself
Upon a bridge,
Made of stone.
Watching
The flames return.
Standing between,
Burning shores.
This bridge,
Cares nothing
For flames.
Fire does not last.
Stone doesn't burn.

~

16

I know the quiet,
Impossible victory,
In that you still,
Have hope.
I know the weight
You heft,
Each time,
You smile.
Like one clean breath,
In a world
Of choking smoke.
I know you.
I've known you before.
You were always
The Light.
I was happy to be,
The Door.

~

17

You
Don't wait
For saviours.
You
Do not pray
For miracles.
You
Become them.

~

18

There's music
In my heart.
Whale song,
In the deep.

It guides me,
Revives me,
It sings me,
To sleep.

Never blames me
For drowning.
Fills my lungs
Helps me breathe.

This whale song,
In my heart.
The echo of god
I got to keep.

~

19

Not the destination
But the quiet place,
You rest and catch
Your breath.

Not in answer, but
Respite, from a world,
Questioning itself,
To death.

Not in night nor day,
But in purple twilight,
When something comes,
As something fades away.

Not in a perfect tomorrow
Or a ruptured past,
But in an eternal now,
Holding an endless today.

Not in pain or panic,
But proud relief.
For the war you fought
Was worth the fight.

Never in sorrow, but
An alchemist's delight.
You turned all that dark,
Into all this light.

~

20

These poems are made
From the things
I wish I could hear,
During my most
Difficult moments,
Curled up on the floor
Wherever I am.
These words that no one
Ever says, that still
Bring music back
To my tuneless feet.

I write them all down,
To remember them,
In case you
Need them too,
Some day.
Curled up,
Wherever you are.

FLAME

SONGS OF MOVEMENT

Flame is energy. It is strength. The stored heat of the sun bursting out of its carbon cage. To rise, to move, to affect the world. Flame is motion.

Everything is moving. Down to atoms, and then further than that. The whole universe is dancing, and we are dancing along with it. Even when we are sitting absolutely still, we are still hurtling through space.

Movement is life, because the universe is constantly in motion. Deeper than being in motion. It *is* motion. Every particle of us is in constant motion.

Aren't we happiest dancing, playing outdoors and generally just racing about? I believe the greatest advantage children have over adults, which is directly related to happiness, is that they are always in motion.

As you grow, the frequency of ecstatic motion, more often than not, gets rarer and rarer. Inversely, the level of despondency and malaise increase. Children are happier than adults because they move so much more. The same with healthy, active adults, versus those leading more sedentary lives. Be clear these aren't scientific facts based on meticulous research that I have conducted. These are just observations that seem largely accurate, based on everything I've observed in the people around me.

Of course, I don't mean to suggest that staying still, or immobile, is a totally wrong thing. Of course not. We are all children of inertia. My favourite activities are solitary and stationary: writing and sketching. But then, when you think about it, they aren't still activities either. They are kinetic and feverish and joyfully exhausting when I get in the zone and get going. The hand is leaping about a page, the fingers are click-clacking away, and my mind might as well be a cosmic superhighway.

The Flame, I mean, is much deeper than simple locomotion. The Flame is the divine spark of life, breathed into my clay by the universe. It is the first essential thing in me. Beneath everything else that makes me Me, I am a spark. A flicker of cosmic fire.

The feeling when I'm in tune with that fire, when it is filling my body and energizing me, is when I know I am healthiest. Being able to do something. Anything. I've heard therapists and psychiatrists prescribe simple chores like cleaning, ironing, dusting as a kind of medicine for depression and despondency. Start moving the physical body, and the mind and the spirit will have no choice but to rise and tag along.

This is why, now, when I read a poem of mine that carries a flame, I know I'm at or back on my way to a positive place. I know I'm past the worst of the hurt and I am healing. I know I made it through. When my poems start dancing, I know I'm ready to dance again too. When my poems have fire, I know I'll be okay. Because I'm burning, again.

And I, am made of fire.

01

Melt me today,
Into the sunset.
Take me away
With you tonight.
Don't leave me alone
With the darkness.
Take me wherever
You take the Light.

~

02

If we could only,
Hold ourselves,
Each other,
Gently,
Hold each other
Still.
Perhaps then,
Our jagged edges
Wouldn't make
Us bleed.
But human as we are,
We just can't stop,
Thrashing.
With this
Ceaseless want,
To be more . . .
This impossible need.

~

03

I crawl
Towards
The Light,
One poem
At a time.
The darkness
Will not
Claim me.
I will not
Fall behind.

~

04

I'm just a clown.
Broken, but merry.
Who learnt to dance,
The year they
Outlawed the music.
But hush now.
I remember the steps.
You can hum us the tune.
And we can dance
A little revolution
Together,
In the pocket Universe,
Of this little room.

~

05

I'm not afraid
Of failure.
Or gravity.
I am not
Afraid
To fall.
I'm afraid
I'll be mediocre.
That I'll never,
Even try to fly,
At all.

~

06

There is a boy,
On Juhu beach,
Flying a kite,
Higher and
Steadier than
I've ever seen.
I wish,
I could make
Of my heart,
A kite.
Ask that boy,
'I can't stand
The ground
Any more.
Boy, won't you
Please,
Do the same,
With me?'

~

07

A particle of light,
Barely a remnant,
That I hold tight
Inside me.
To shelter through,
The dark and the gloom,
Like a child.

Until my final day,
When it no longer,
Needs me to stay,
For it can shine,
Without me now.
And I can rest,
For a while.

~

08

I think
That it's a test.
To see,
If given a meagre
Mortal lifetime,
Confined
To this tiny
Blue pearl,
Cast out
To be consumed
By the oceans
Of space,
Will we manage
To recall,
The true shape of us?
To regain,
At least some,
Of our infinity.

~

09

I've learnt
To trace,
Silver linings,
Around all the clouds
That come and go.
I've learnt
To face
The truest me,
The one
I was sent,
To get to know.

~

10

I'm stranded
In the dark,
Yearning
For a light,
I've never seen.

I'm branded
By this spark,
Burning
To be the man,
I've never been.

They bound me
To this body.
Chained me
To this place.

Ever since I
Began to dream,
I dream only,
Of escape.

~

11

So it goes,
The light falls,
On all of us,
And we learn,
To drink it in.
So that when
Darkness comes,
As darkness must,
We can be lit,
From within.

~

12

They will give you
A label.
To demean or flatter.
A chain to make you,
Easier to handle.
But you are
Neither the light,
Nor the shadow cast.
You are simply
the candle.
I know we long to be
Movement and fury.
To dance,
To shine,
To soar.
But the beauty
Of who you are,
Is revealed when you
Cease trying
To be the dancer.
And grow as humble,
And still as the floor.

~

13

Every heart has a song,
Known long before
It ever learnt
How to beat.
Few will be those
Who can ever hear
Your secret song.
Fewer still, those who
Will call it sweet.
You will move
Through life looking
For the ones
Who can sing along,
To the melody of you.
But know this my friend,
You are not a song
That shall go unsung.
Every breath you take
Is a pure note, pealing
Clear and true.
And long after
Your flesh and memory

Have faded,
Those notes will linger.
Until all songs are sung
And we can return
To where the songs come from.

~

14

I read the books
They told me to read.
I listened to those
They said I should heed.
I did the things
They said I should do.
Chased the things
They said I would need.

Not a whisper,
Not a hint,
Not an echo,
Of an answer
That mattered,
That was true.
Then I listened,
In exhausted
Silence,
To the quiet voice
Of my own heart.
I felt it make
A hallowed temple,

Of an empty room.
Now I dance
To my own Music
Now I howl
At the Moon.

~

15

It finds me.
Even when
I do not seek it.
Even when
I don't believe
It even exists
At all.
It finds me.
When I grow weak,
It knows.
It comes,
Like the absolute
Stillness,
Of an unstruck chord,
That knows,
With utter certainty,
One day
It shall be strummed.

~

16

Do not seek,
To be still.
Dance.
Be as you were
Before this.
Untampered,
Untamed.
Be tempest.
Untempered,
Unchained,
In peals of thunder.
Cry out,
'I am sure!'
You are free
To be you.
Be still
Nevermore.

~

17

Do not merely
Strut and fret,
And waste,
Your brief hour,
Upon the stage.
Sing and dance.
Leap and twirl.
Every atom
Is a dervish.
You were made,
To whirl.

~

18

Fools will be wise.
The wise will remember
How it felt to be fools.

The lonely will be loved.
The Ocean will finally
Get to kiss the Moon.

You know me deeply.
I know the shape of all
The aches that're you.

We're doing all right,
And looking mighty fine,
Doing it too.

It's all just a dance, and
We do so love dancing,
No matter the tune.

~

SPIRIT

SONGS OF LIGHT AND DARK, OF ME AND YOU

My understanding of the Spirit and spirituality, or rather my thoughts (for I can't really claim to 'understand' it), have over the years become steeped in Zen and Sufi philosophy. The more I live and learn, the more intrinsic and self-sustaining that kind of thinking gets.

Specifically, the idea of dialectical or dualistic monism, which holds that all of our reality is actually one unified whole. A whole that expresses itself in dualistic terms: like light and dark, etc. For the dualistic monist, the essential unity of all reality is at once also that of complementary polarities, which, although seeming opposed in the realm of experience and perception, are consubstantial in a transcendent sense. Everything is everything else. Everything is itself, too. At the same time. Including good and evil. Including you and me.

One of the most ubiquitous symbols for this philosophy is the tai chi, or the yin-yang, from ancient Chinese philosophy. A circle divided by a sinuous line, one half dark with a white eye, the other half white, with a dark eye. In each there is the other. In light there is some darkness, and in darkness there is light. They define each other, sustain each other, and exist at the same time, as one thing. In separateness we are united. In union we are rendered distinct.

We are increasingly living in a world that's so fiercely individualistic and egocentric, that kindness and empathy are being bred out of us. We are incapable any more; worse, unwilling to even entertain the idea of complexity, much less duality. Everything must be what we need it to be. Only what we believe. Everything has to agree with me. With people like me. Especially people like me. Look at how unique and unlike anyone else we are. We are special. We must be special, our invisible 'guy in the sky' said so. We, my brothers and sisters, with our shared ideology, we are special. But of course, I'm more special than the rest of you. I'm super special.

This world, full of extremes and extremists, is getting harder and harder to keep a gentle balance in. The need for spirituality and spiritual awakening is, I believe, the second most important thing to collectively undertake, right after we try to stop murdering the planet. I know I sound like Russell Brand right now, and I will claim it as a compliment. I love him. And he's right about this. So is the trainload of people around the world who have been cautioning us over the years.

It has taken a long time for me to learn to constantly keep in check the balance between the light and dark aspects of me. To keep in a healthy check, the boundaries between me and another, while at the same time accepting and respecting all the ways in which we are the same. More than balance, is the understanding that even in singular concepts, there can be complexity of meaning.

Light can be life-giving, yet can scorch and leave nothing but dust to be blown away. Light can be comforting and illuminating, pushing back the shadows of fear and ignorance. Or it can be harsh, like the light shined into the terrified eyes of an innocent man strapped to a chair, awaiting torture. It can reveal or it can blind. It can illuminate or it can shame. It can grow, or it can blight.

Darkness can be terrifying—the utter absence of light, being alone (or not alone) in the dark, are among the fears that are seared into humanity's genes. Evil people commit evil deeds at night (of course, that's simplified, but I'm saying this to illuminate the common connotations). It is a time of monsters and dark magic.

It can also be comforting. After a long day spent in the harsh light of the sun, to lie in the cool darkness is one of the greatest feelings. We are swallowed by darkness when we sleep. Darkness knows our dreams. Darkness is a sign that the day is done, along with all the trials and hardships it might have brought. Tomorrow the light will return and you can try again.

I love that old Native American parable of the two wolves constantly at war in our hearts. One is Evil; anger, envy, sorrow, regret, ego, etc. Darkness. The other is Good; peace, love, serenity, empathy, etc. Light. The one that wins is the one you feed. And that victory is never permanent or final. You don't kill the other. You can't. It's as much a part of you as your skin. As much a part of each other. But you can affect which one is stronger in you. Which one stays stronger.

As I have started to imbibe and practise these teachings, I have noticed a great improvement in my ability to handle the complexities that exist between Me and You. The Self, and the Other. The differences that separate and define us. The similarities that make each one thing. The same thing, part of one system, parts of a unified whole. The things that keep us together. The things that push us apart, can all be found in the grey margins between you and me.

All the issues and struggles I have with people, socially and in deeper, more intimate relationships, all have to do with my navigating the fickle and shifting minefield of overlapping egos.

Where do you and I converge? What are the areas, ideas where we will never meet? Is it even so important to know these things? Are you a human being like me? Why do we let so many banal differences and factors come between us when we are essentially the exact same creature?

I survived the elemental years. And though I know that many elemental storms will find me over the course of my life (that's life. It never stops coming for you), I'm comfortable in my skin now. Confident in my spirit. I know I am capable of dealing with them all, picking up the pieces and reforging myself if they ever manage to break me again.

I believe light and dark, you and I, are in superposition, and in a constant, never-ending ebb and flow between each other. Not only do we all occupy the same fraction of space-time, I believe we *tend* to occupy the same position. We are supposed to be this part of the whole. We are supposed to be this part of each other.

SONGS OF LIGHT. SONGS OF YOU.

Think of a bird
Freewheeling
Across a winter sky,
Only to alight,
For a flicker of time,
Beside you,
To cock its head
To chirp at you,
Then flit away,
Message delivered.
If just the thought
Of that bird
Brought
A little respite
To your tumult,
And a smile
To your face,
Then,
I wrote
All of these poems
For you.

~

02

I am of the Mountain.
I am of the breeze.
I am of the burning.
I am of the Sea.
I am what you touch,
I am what you dream.
I am of the stars, and
The emptiness between.
I am of you, Darling,
And you, are of me.

~

03

Just know,
Your secret fears,
Your secret shame,
I share them too.

They don't need to be,
Secrets any more.
You know me.
I know you.

~

04

You,
Are what
You've been
Seeking.
You,
Are why
You haven't
Found it,
Yet.

~

05

I want you to know,
I feel it too.
All of it.
All of the time.
You may feel alone,
And you might be,
But,
You are not
Unknown.
Not to me.

~

06

This is
A difficult place
To be.
A difficult time
To go through.
But,
I am glad
To be here.
Gladder still,
To be here,
With you.

~

07

You have lost faith,
Before.
You have despaired.
Despite your many blessings,
You have despised
The very air.
You have wandered,
Past the borders
Of the abyss.
Felt the very ground
Fall away,
Felt something squeeze
Your heart, and twist.
But you're still here.
And you have learnt
To feel glad you exist.
Every morning
You count the reasons.
Every morning itself,
You add to the list.

Life's full of bigger,
Flashier battles,
But none as important
As this.

~

08

They will try,
To teach you,
You never had,
Any wings.
For they fear,
You flying away,
From all these
Broken things.
Flying away
From them.

~

09

You won't
Find it with
Your mind.
That's just
A mirror.
You must
Look through
Your spirit.
That
Is your
Window.

~

10

They'll let you in,
If you stop being you.
If you agree to become,
Who they want you to.
Just know this . . .
If you stay true,
One day soon,
You won't need
Them to.
You'll see the miracle,
That you
Were always meant
To be you.

~

11

Everyone knows,
Except for you.
Everyone can,
Except you.
Everyone's invited,
Except you.
But then,
No one else,
Is you.
You win.

~

12

It is your duty,
To say to the world,
All the things,
You wish someone
Had said to you.
It is your dharma,
To fight the world,
In all the wars,
You wish had been
Fought for you.

~

13

Why are you hell-bent
On self-destruction?
Why do you scuttle
Your own self-esteem?
Why is your rage,
Always pointed inward?
How can mere failure,
Be brighter
Than the Dream?
So they took away
Your dignity.
So you had
To compromise.
Now you avoid
All mirrors.
Now you dress
Only in disguise.
Gather up these
Remnants and cast them
Down the drain.
They are just pieces
Of your chains.

You are stronger now,
Than what you were,
Because of what remains.

~

14

You are defined,
Not by your history,
Nor the victories
You seek to earn.
You are named
By what defeats you
What makes you weep
The fires in which
You burn.

~

15

Do not wait,
For others,
To give you
The answers
You seek.
They do not
Know,
The questions,
That matter
To you.
We are made
To be
Our own
Destinies.
We have all
Been chosen.
We are all
Prophecies
Coming true.

~

16

You feel lost.
Not because you
Are not where
You wished to be,
But because
You're not who,
You should have been.
But,
You're breathing, yes?
Then,
There is still time.

~

17

This.
All of this,
Is a temple.
And you,
Your life,
Are the prayer.

~

18

It does exist.
When you
Finally accept,
That you
Have been
Worthy of it,
All this time.
It will find you.
I promise you.
You just have to
Believe.

~

19

Life,
Hunts down
All of us.
Until you show it,
That although
You are not
A hunter,
You, most certainly,
Are not
Prey.

~

20

Tell me the name
Of the God,
Who saw you
Through the trauma.
Who walked you
Through the flames.
Who led you to me,
Taught me
The miracle
Of your name.
Teach me about
That God.
So I can know,
True worship,
Again.

~

21

Do not waste
Any more time,
Seeking affirmation,
From this faithless crowd,
Amidst whom you knew,
You never belonged.
You know the place
You deserve to be,
The life you've been
Hoping to find.
It is on its way,
My friend.
Just, hold on.

~

22

You are not
Your aching body.
You are divine light
Caught in a dream.
You are not even
What you look like.
You are what is felt,
When you are seen.

~

23

There should be
No clear boundary
Between you and I.
Like a river
Meeting the sea,
No clear line
Separating
What is given,
What is taken
Away.

~

24

Love is a bird.
Flying high,
Flying free.

And if you
Cannot be
The breeze,

You must learn
How to be
The tree.

~

25

This black
And white world,
Doesn't know
What to do,
With your
Technicolour soul.
To it everything
Looks the same
Lifeless grey.
Only you
Can see the colours
That matter to you.

~

26

When,
The bridges fall,
I want you
To remember:
You were never
What they
Connected.
You were
And will always
Be the water.

~

27

Love is not the answer,
It's the question
You must live
Your entire life,
Studying,
Trying to understand.
The answer is
What comes after.

~

28

Life isn't the ship,
Nor some perfect destination.
It isn't the contents of the hold.
Their value in summation.
It is the storm.
That will wreck your little boat
Drag you out to sea.
It is the current that carries you
To that uncharted shore,
Where you were always,
Meant to be.

~

29

You have wandered
Deserts
of discontent.
Stumbling,
Heat-struck.
Seeing futures
Shimmer
In and out of view.
You have stumbled
Through deserts
of despair,
Trying to keep,
The Betrayal
Of mirages from
Cleaving your heart
In two.
You have come far enough.
You can stop here.
If you choose.

You can become
Your own oasis
Your own refuge
You can stay here,
If you dare.
Let the world
Now wander
Into you.

~

30

Even
In blinding light,
Shadows still,
Remain.
Shadows
Are the edges
Shadows
Are the frame.
But in a world,
Of ash and shade,
Remember, you
Are a flame.

~

31

They crack your heart
They fragment
Your feelings.
You can't tell any more
If you're hurting
Or you're healing.

Rescue is only
For the truly lost
They say.

Not for those
Of us still
Losing our way.

So here we are,
Punch-drunk fools.
Still reeling.
And here we'll remain.
Hope-mad loons
Still believing.

~

SONGS OF THE DARK. SONGS OF THE SELF.

01

When I write,
I am a traveller,
Gazing at a dying fire.
Sleeping in the wild,
Many miles from shelter,
Under the trees and
Their lullaby choir.
Though I am alone,
And no one can find me,
This solitude is more precious
Than all the riches
Wandering the highway.
When I write I become
Part of what is never born,
And what shall never have to die.
I am what the Universe dreams of,
What puts the stars in the sky.

~

02

I look and feel normal,
But I think I lost my mind.
Somewhere,
Without realizing it,
I got nudged out of line.
I waited so long
For the Miracle,
I missed every other sign.
Now there's nothing really
To sing about,
No victory bells to chime.
These words
Will be the only proof,
That I reached out,
Desperately hoping,
God would reach out
In kind.
Trapped in the lonely dark,
Like me
Both of us desperate
To shine.

~

03

If I fail,
At this, and,
I know I might,
Let it be
So spectacularly,
I go insane.
I want them,
The faithless,
The benumbed,
To know that I
Dared enough,
That I
Cared enough,
To dig that deep,
In the end.

~

04

I know,
It is not easy,
Being merely human.
Trapped in a cage,
Of flesh and bone.
I know
You remember,
You were a fire,
Bright enough
To light the cosmos
Alone.

———————

~

05

I love the Moon most,
When I see it,
Faint and unassuming,
In the daytime sky.
Lingering
Like a guardian.
Promising that at least
Through that night,
It will be there
To help you
Find your way,
Through the dark.
I think of love,
And of faith,
Like I think,
Of moonlight.

~

06

I,
Am but
A candle,
In the rain.
But oh,
How I dream,
Of being,
The lightning.

~

07

Sorrow claimed me,
Long ago.
It led me where
I needed to be,
It knew the secrets,
I needed to know.
It helped me forgive
My yesterdays,
It helped me
Fill hope
In Tomorrow.
Joy was ever
A heedless rush,
Into the giddy arms,
Of the sea.
Sorrow was the shore,
Waiting patiently for me.
It is the blessed cup,
From which these poems
Are poured.

Joys are never taken
For granted
By the children
Of sorrow.

~

08

I thought
I was a river,
Racing to find
My ocean.
To leap into
To finally know
How it feels
To be at peace.
Now
I am older,
I hurt
Like a soldier,
Now at last,
I can see.
I am the ocean,
It is the rivers
That empty
Into me.

~

09

I know
I have been
Made for
The Rising.

No matter
How often
In life,
I fall down,

In my
Secret heart,
I'm always
Flying.

In my soul
I've never
Even felt
The ground.

~

10

I am boundless,
Tonight.
The edges of me,
Stretch out far
Beyond the horizon.
All that lives,
Lives in me.
All that breathes,
Breathes with me.
All that loves,
All that despairs.
All the predators,
All the doves.
Move in me.
I am boundless,
Tonight.
Tomorrow
The world will remind me
That I am only myself.

~

11

I am never lonely.
Every younger me,
Everyone I'll ever be,
Surrounds me.
And finally, we are all
Fast friends.

I am never lonely.
But I wish you existed,
To show me, it exists.
That it had found me.
I wish it was true.
And would never end.

But I'm never lonely.
We take our own
Hands, and we dance
Around me.
Until reality smiles,
And shrugs, and bends.

~

12

I am
Meant to be,
Wrapped within
This particular moment.
Awake inside
This particular mind.
Afire inside
This particular skin.
Alive in this
Particular time.
I am,
Meant to be,
Entirely,
Me.

~

13

I've read,
Trying to find
The Divine
By thinking,
Is like trying
To empty the Ocean
With a spoon.

And yet,
Here I am,
Cutlery in hand,
Alone on
An empty beach.
Being laughed at
By the Moon.

But I don't mind.
Pretty soon, I know
I'll be laughing too.

~

14

I have stumbled,
Through darkness,
To dance again,
In the Light
Of day.

I have shed
What wasn't true,
To gather again
The truths I want
To say.

Now the words
Surround me
Like the Ocean.
The poems come
In waves.

~

15

I've always had a soft spot for trouble.
Always had a high threshold for pain.

I almost drowned once, in deep water.
Yet every chance, I'm paddling back out again.

This will be my only life. At least, at the end,
The only one I'll hopefully, be able to recall.

So I gamble everything I have. It's mine to lose,
And before I go, I intend to lose it all.

I'll take nothing with me, that anyone had to give.
Just the smile in my spirit. And the scars of a life well-lived.

~

16

I stopped waiting,
For a star to fall.
Some final sign
To come into view.

I am just
Doing the work now.
Whether or not
Dreams come true.

The work
Is the purpose
The Victory
Dance, too.

I am happy.
In my night sky,
The Moon,
Is always blue.

~

17

There is
Not a day,
That the dark
Doesn't find me.

And,

There is
Never a day,
That the Light
Doesn't drive it,

Away.

18

Where do I begin?
You begin where
You ended.
Where you had to stop
Out of excuses
And winded.
You begin
Wherever you are.

Where do I go?
You go where
You haven't been.
Dust off your spirit
Let it take you
For a spin.
Go wherever you can
No matter how far.

You'll still be you.
At every rest and rising.
Through every single test.
You'll still be you.
And you my friend
Are blessed.

Acknowledgements

There are far too many people I am grateful to, so I'm just going to stick with the ones directly responsible for this book.

Asha Hariharan. Pramod Menon. Bernd Pflug.

Whatever spark of creativity I might have come into this world with, you made sure that spark fanned aflame. My love for the English language and my desire to write would definitely not have survived the banal, wordless little tyrannies of this world, without your nurturing. You were the greatest teachers. I love you all.

The lovely people at Penguin Random House India, particularly Radhika Marwah. Thank you for your faith, patience (because it can't be easy dealing with a wanderer who has a genuine distaste for mobile phones) and generosity. You are the reason this book exists at all. You made my dream come true.

Antra K. For the gorgeous artwork. You gave me the exact cover I didn't know I wanted. You are a wonder. Also very patient, for aforementioned reasons.

Ralph Rebello. The Editor (the 'E' is always capital), who went through my poems with the surest, gentlest hand.

Getting rid of all the myriad little errors, without ever touching the poem. Thank you.

And last, but certainly not least, not in this beating heart of mine:

You. Who are holding this book in your hands. All these words were meant for you.

You. Who have been reading and supporting me on Instagram all these years. In an Internet asphyxiating with content, you continued to read my work, and not one of you has ever been unkind. It's a world full of trolls, and I don't have a single one. Because you are the people you are. And you are blessings.

You. Who'd never read a word I'd written before this book. Thank you for picking it up. I hope you enjoyed some of what you read, flipping through to get to this sentence. I hope to see you again.